WWW.BLACKLEGACYPRESS.ORG

SLAVE NARRATIVES

ADMINISTRATIVE FILES

By
United States.
Work Projects Administration

ISBN: 978-1-63652-218-0

SLAVE NARRATIVES

A Folk History of Slavery in the United States.
From Interviews with Former Slaves

UNITED STATES.
WORK PROJECTS ADMINISTRATION

TYPEWRITTEN RECORDS PREPARED BY
THE FEDERAL WRITERS' PROJECT
1936-1938
ASSEMBLED BY
THE LIBRARY OF CONGRESS PROJECT
WORK PROJECTS ADMINISTRATION
FOR THE DISTRICT OF COLUMBIA
SPONSORED BY THE LIBRARY OF
CONGRESS

WASHINGTON 1941

ADMINISTRATIVE FILES

Prepared by
Federal Works Agency
Work Projects Administration
For The District Of Columbia

CONTENTS

INTRODUCTION

I

This collection of slave narratives had its beginning in the second year of the former Federal Writers' Project (now the Writers' Program), 1936, when several state Writers' Projects—notably those of Florida, Georgia, and South Carolina—recorded interviews with ex-slaves residing in those states. On April 22, 1937, a standard questionnaire for field workers drawn up by John A. Lomax, then National Advisor on Folklore and Folkways for the Federal Writers' Project[1], was issued from Washington as "Supplementary Instructions #9-E to The American Guide Manual" (appended below). Also associated with the direction and criticism of the work in the Washington office of the Federal Writers' Project were Henry G. Alsberg, Director; George Cronyn, Associate Director; Sterling A. Brown, Editor on Negro Affairs; Mary Lloyd, Editor; and B.A. Botkin, Folklore Editor succeeding Mr. Lomax.[2]

[1] Mr. Lomax served from June 25, 1936, to October 23, 1937, with a ninety-day furlough beginning July 24, 1937. According to a memorandum written by Mr. Alsberg on March 23, 1937, Mr. Lomax was "in charge of the collection of folklore all over the United States for the Writers' Project. In connection with this work he is making recordings of Negro songs and cowboy ballads. Though technically on the payroll of the Survey of Historical Records, his work is done for the Writers and the results will make several national

volumes of folklore. The essays in the State Guides devoted to folklore are also under his supervision." Since 1933 Mr. Lomax has been Honorary Curator of the Archive of American Folk Song, Library of Congress.

[2] Folklore Consultant, from May 2 to July 31, 1938; Folklore Editor, from August 1, 1938, to August 31, 1939.

On August 31, 1939, the Federal Writers' Project became the Writers' Program, and the National Technical Project in Washington was terminated. On October 17, the first Library of Congress Project, under the sponsorship of the Library of Congress, was set up by the Work Projects Administration in the District of Columbia, to continue some of the functions of the National Technical Project, chiefly those concerned with books of a regional or nationwide scope. On February 12, 1940, the project was reorganized along strictly conservation lines, and on August 16 it was succeeded by the present Library of Congress Project (Official Project No. 165-2-26-7, Work Project No. 540).

The present Library of Congress Project, under the sponsorship of the Library of Congress, is a unit of the Public Activities Program of the Community Service Programs of the Work Projects Administration for the District of Columbia. According to the Project Proposal (WPA Form 301), the purpose of the Project is to "collect, check, edit, index, and otherwise prepare for use WPA records, Professional and Service Projects."

The Writers' Unit of the Library of Congress Project processes material left over from or not needed for publication by the state Writers' Projects. On file in the Washington office in August, 1939, was a large body of slave narratives, photographs of former slaves, interviews with white informants regarding slavery, transcripts of laws, advertisements, records of sale, transfer, and manumission of slaves, and other documents. As unpublished manuscripts of the Federal Writers' Project these records passed into the hands of the Library of Congress Project for processing; and from them has been assembled the present collection of some two thousand narratives from the following seventeen states: Alabama, Arkansas, Florida, Georgia, Indiana, Kansas, Kentucky, Maryland, Mississippi, Missouri, North Carolina, Ohio, Oklahoma, South Carolina, Tennessee, Texas, and Virginia[1].

[1] The bulk of the Virginia narratives is still in the state office. Excerpts from these are included in The Negro in Virginia, compiled by Workers of the Writers' Program of the Work Projects Administration in the State of Virginia, Sponsored by the Hampton Institute, Hastings House, Publishers, New York, 1940. Other slave narratives are published in Drums and Shadows, Survival Studies among the Georgia Coastal Negroes, Savannah Unit, Georgia Writers' Project, Work Projects Administration, University of Georgia Press, 1940. A composite article, "Slaves," based on excerpts from three interviews, was contributed by Elizabeth Lomax to the American Stuff issue of Direction, Vol. 1, No. 3, 1935.

The work of the Writers' Unit in preparing the narratives for deposit in the Library of Congress consisted principally of arranging the manuscripts and photographs by states and alphabetically by informants within the states, listing the informants and illustrations, and collating the contents in seventeen volumes divided into thirty-three parts. The following material has been omitted: Most of the interviews with informants born too late to remember anything of significance regarding slavery or concerned chiefly with folklore; a few negligible fragments and unidentified manuscripts; a group of Tennessee interviews showing evidence of plagiarism; and the supplementary material gathered in connection with the narratives. In the course of the preparation of these volumes, the Writers' Unit compiled data for an essay on the narratives and partially completed an index and a glossary. Enough additional material is being received from the state Writers' Projects, as part of their surplus, to make a supplement, which, it is hoped, will contain several states not here represented, such as Louisiana.

All editing had previously been done in the states or the Washington office. Some of the pencilled comments have been identified as those of John A. Lomax and Alan Lomax, who also read the manuscripts. In a few cases, two drafts or versions of the same interview have been included for comparison of interesting variations or alterations.

II

Set beside the work of formal historians, social scientists, and novelists, slave autobiographies, and contemporary records of abolitionists and planters, these life histories, taken down as far as possible in the narrators' words, constitute an invaluable body of unconscious evidence or indirect source material, which scholars and writers dealing with the South, especially social psychologists and cultural anthropologists, cannot afford to reckon without. For the first and the last time, a large number of surviving slaves (many of whom have since died) have been permitted to tell their own story, in their own way. In spite of obvious limitations—bias and fallibility of both informants and interviewers, the use of leading questions, unskilled techniques, and insufficient controls and checks—this saga must remain the most authentic and colorful source of our knowledge of the lives and thoughts of thousands of slaves, of their attitudes toward one another, toward their masters, mistresses, and overseers, toward poor whites, North and South, the Civil War, Emancipation, Reconstruction, religion, education, and virtually every phase of Negro life in the South.

The narratives belong to folk history—history recovered from the memories and lips of participants or eye-witnesses, who mingle group with individual experience and both with observation, hearsay, and tradition. Whether the narrators relate what they actually saw and thought and felt, what they imagine, or what they have thought and felt about slavery since, now we know why they thought and felt as they did. To the white myth of slavery must be added the slaves' own folklore and folk-say of slavery. The patterns they reveal are folk and regional patterns—the patterns of field hand, house and body servant, and artisan; the patterns of kind and cruel master or mistress; the patterns of Southeast and Southwest, lowland and upland, tidewater and inland, smaller and larger plantations, and racial mixture (including Creole and Indian).

The narratives belong also to folk literature. Rich not only in folk songs, folk tales, and folk speech but also in folk humor and poetry, crude or skilful in dialect, uneven in tone and treatment, they constantly reward one with earthy imagery, salty phrase, and sensitive detail. In their unconscious art, exhibited in many a fine and powerful short story, they are a contribution to the realistic writing of the Negro. Beneath all the surface contradictions and exaggerations, the fantasy and flattery, they possess an essential truth and humanity which surpasses as it supplements history and literature.

Washington, D.C.
June 12, 1941

B.A. Botkin
Chief Editor, Writers' Unit
Library of Congress Project

BEARING ON THE HISTORY OF THE SLAVE NARRATIVES

From the correspondence and memoranda files of the Washington office of the Federal Writers' Project the following instructions and criticisms relative to the slave narrative collection, issued from April 1 to September 8, 1937, have been selected. They throw light on the progress of the work, the development of materials and methods, and some of the problems encountered.

1. Copy of Memorandum from George Cronyn to Mrs. Eudora R. Richardson. April 1, 1937.

2. Autograph Memorandum from John A. Lomax to George Cronyn. April 9, 1937. [Handwritten version, Typewritten version']

3. Copy of Memorandum from George Cronyn to Edwin Bjorkman, enclosing a Memorandum from John A. Lomax on "Negro Dialect Suggestions." April 14, 1937.

4. Mimeographed "Supplementary Instructions #9-E to the American Guide Manual. Folklore. Stories from Ex-Slaves."April 22, 1937. Prepared by John A. Lomax.

5. Copy of Memorandum from George Cronyn to Edwin Bjorkman. May 3, 1937.

6. Copy of Memorandum from Henry G. Alsberg to State Directors of the Federal Writers' Project. June 9, 1937.

7. Copy of "Notes by an Editor on Dialect Usage in Accounts by Interviews with Ex-Slaves." June 20, 1937. Prepared by Sterling A. Brown.

8. Copy of Memorandum from Henry G. Alsberg to State Directors of the Federal Writers' Project. July 30, 1937.

9. Copy of Memorandum from Henry G. Alsberg to State Directors of the Federal Writers' Project. September 8, 1937.

[File 1]
Sent to: NORTH & SOUTH CAROLINA, GEORGIA, ALABAMA,
LOUISIANA, TEXAS, ARKANSAS, TENNESSEE,
KENTUCKY, MISSOURI, MISSISSIPPI, OKLA.

April 1, 1937

Mrs. Eudora R. Richardson, Acting State Director
Federal Writers' Project, WPA
Rooms 321-4, American Bank Building
Richmond, Virginia

Subj: Folklore

NORTH & SOUTH CAROLINA, GEORGIA, ALABAMA

Dear Mrs. Richardson:

We have received from Florida a remarkably interesting collection of autobiographical stories by ex-slaves. Such documentary records by the survivors of a historic period in America are invaluable, both to the student of history and to creative writers.

If a volume of such importance can be assembled we will endeavor to secure its publication. There undoubtedly is material of this sort to be found in your State by making the proper contact through tactful interviewers. While it is desirable to give a running story of the life of each subject, the color and human interest will be greatly enhanced if it is told largely in the words of the person interviewed. The peculiar idiom is often more expressive than a literary account.

We shall be very glad to know if you have undertaken any research of this sort, or plan to do so.

Very truly yours,
 George Cronyn
 Associate Director
 Federal Writers' Project

GWCronyn/a

[File 2: Handwritten version]

4/9/1937

[illegible] Cronyn:

In replying to this letter I would like for you to ~~[illegible]~~ [illegible] especially two stories:

1. Ida Henningan by Sarah H. Hall, Athens, Ga.

2. Uncle Willis, Miss Velma Bell, Supervisor, Athens, Ga.

The stories are worth while be[illegible] [illegible] two are [illegible] (exceptionally) in dialect and abound in human interest [illegible] All the interviewers stand by the Negro expressions. I would prefer to [illegible] and [illegible]

[File 2: Typewritten version]

[illegible] (not typed) interviews," and I
would like to see as soon
as possible all the work for
[illegible] Miss Dillard [illegible]
It is most important
to secure copies of "Slave
tales, sea stories and the
like." This item is new and
all the states should send
in similar material.
Yours,
[illegible]

(Transcript of Preceding Autograph Memorandum)
4/9/37

PRECEDING AUTOGRAPH MEMORANDUM

Mr. Cronyn:

In replying to this letter I should like for you to commend especially two stories:

1. Lula Flannigan by Sarah H. Hall Athens, Ga.

2. Uncle Willis, Miss Velma Bell, Supervisor, Athens, Ga.

All the stories are worth while but these two are mainly (one entirely) in dialect and abound in human interest touches. All the interviewers should copy the Negro expressions.

I much prefer to read unedited (but typed) "interviews," and I should like to see as soon as possible all the seventy-five to which Miss Dillard refers.

It is most important, too, to secure copies of "slave codes, overseers codes and the like." This item is new and all the states should send in similar material.

Yours,
 John A. Lomax

[File 3]
Sent to: North and South Carolina, Georgia,
Alabama, Louisiana, Texas, Arkansas,
Tennessee, Kentucky, Missouri,
Mississippi, Oklahoma.

April 14, 1937

Mr. Edwin Bjorkman
State Director, Federal Writers' Project
Works Progress Administration
City Hall, Fifth Floor
Asheville, North Carolina

NORTH AND SOUTH CAROLINA, GEORGIA

Dear Mr. Bjorkman:

We have received more stories of ex-slaves and are gratified by the quality and interest of the narratives. Some of these stories have been accompanied by photographs of the subjects. We would like to have portraits wherever they can be secured, but we urge your photographers to make the studies as simple, natural, and "unposed" as possible. Let the background, cabin or whatnot, be the normal setting—in short, just the picture a visitor would expect to find by "dropping in" on one of these old-timers.

Enclosed is a memorandum of Mr. Lomax with suggestions for simplifying the spelling of certain recurring dialect words. This does not mean that the interviews should be entirely in "straight English"—simply, that we want them to be more readable to those uninitiated in the broadest Negro speech.

Very truly yours,

George Cronyn
 Associate Director
 Federal Writers' Project

GWCronyn:MEB

This paragraph was added to the letter to Arkansas.

Mr. Lomax is very eager to get such records as you mention: Court Records of Sale, Transfer, and Freeing of Slaves, as well as prices paid.

Negro Dialect Suggestions (Stories of Ex-Slaves)

Do not write:

Ah for I

Poe for po' (poor)

Hit for it

Tuh for to

Wuz for was

Baid for bed

Daid for dead

Ouh for our

Mah for my

Ovah for over

Othuh for other

Wha for whar (where)

Undah for under

Fuh for for

Yondah for yonder

Moster for marster or massa

Gwainter for gwineter (going to)

Oman for woman

Ifn for iffen (if)

Fiuh or fiah for fire

Uz or uv or o' for of

Poar for poor or po'

J'in for jine

Coase for cose

Utha for other

Yo' for you

Gi' for give

Cot for caught

Kin' for kind

Cose for 'cause

Tho't for thought

[File 4]
WORKS PROGRESS ADMINISTRATION
Federal Writers' Project
1500 Eye St. N.W.
Washington, D.C.

SUPPLEMENTARY INSTRUCTIONS #9-E
To
THE AMERICAN GUIDE MANUAL

FOLKLORE
STORIES FROM EX-SLAVES

WORKS PROGRESS ADMINISTRATION

Note: In some states it may be possible to locate only a very few ex-slaves, but an attempt should be made in every state. Interesting ex-slave data has recently been reported from Rhode Island, for instance.

April 22, 1937

Stories From Ex-Slaves

The main purpose of these detailed and homely questions is to get the Negro interested in talking about the days of slavery. If he will talk freely, he should be encouraged to say what he pleases without reference to the questions. It should be remembered that the Federal Writers' Project is not interested in taking sides on any question. The worker should not censor any material collected, regardless of its nature.

It will not be necessary, indeed it will probably be a mistake, to ask every person all of the questions. Any incidents or facts he can recall should be written down as nearly as possible just as he says them, but do not use dialect spelling so complicated that it may confuse the reader.

A second visit, a few days after the first one, is important, so that the worker may gather all the worthwhile recollections that the first talk has aroused.

Questions:

1. Where and when were you born?

2. Give the names of your father and mother. Where did they come from? Give names of your brothers and sisters. Tell about your life with them and describe your home and the "quarters." Describe the beds and where you slept. Do you remember anything about your grandparents or any stories told you about them?

3. What work did you do in slavery days? Did you ever earn any money? How? What did you buy with this money?

4. What did you eat and how was it cooked? Any possums? Rabbits? Fish? What food did you like best? Did the slaves have their own gardens?

5. What clothing did you wear in hot weather? Cold weather? On Sundays? Any shoes? Describe your wedding clothes.

6. Tell about your master, mistress, their children, the house they lived in, the overseer or driver, poor white neighbors.

7. How many acres in the plantation? How many slaves on it? How and at what time did the overseer wake up the slaves? Did they work hard and late at night? How and for what causes were the slaves punished? Tell what you saw. Tell some of the stories you heard.

8. Was there a jail for slaves? Did you ever see any slaves sold or auctioned off? How did groups of slaves travel? Did you ever see slaves in chains?

9. Did the white folks help you to learn to read and write?

10. Did the slaves have a church on your plantation? Did they read the Bible? Who was your favorite preacher? Your favorite spirituals? Tell about the baptizing; baptizing songs. Funerals and funeral songs.

11. Did the slaves ever run away to the North? Why? What did you hear about patrollers? How did slaves carry news from one plantation to another? Did you hear of trouble between the blacks and whites?

12. What did the slaves do when they went to their quarters after the day's work was done on the plantation? Did they work on Saturday afternoons? What did they do Saturday nights? Sundays? Christmas morning? New Year's Day? Any other holidays? Cornshucking? Cotton Picking? Dances? When some of the white master's family married or died? A wedding or death among the slaves?

13. What games did you play as a child? Can you give the words or sing any of the play songs or ring games of the children? Riddles? Charms? Stories about "Raw Head and Bloody Bones" or other "hants" of ghosts? Stories about animals? What do you think of voodoo? Can you give the words or sing any lullabies? Work songs? Plantation

hollers? Can you tell a funny story you have heard or something funny that happened to you? Tell about the ghosts you have seen.

14. When slaves became sick who looked after them? What medicines did tho doctors give them? What medicine (herbs, leaves, or roots) did the slaves use for sickness? What charms did they wear and to keep off what diseases?

15. What do you remember about the war that brought your freedom? What happened on the day news came that you were free? What did your master say and do? When the Yankees came what did they do and say?

16. Tell what work you did and how you lived the first year after the war and what you saw or heard about the KuKlux Klan and the Nightriders. Any school then for Negroes? Any land?

17. Whom did you marry? Describe the wedding. How many children and grandchildren have you and what are they doing?

18. What do you think of Abraham Lincoln? Jefferson Davis? Booker Washington? Any other prominent white man or Negro you have known or heard of?

19. Now that slavery is ended what do you think of it? Tell why you joined a church and why you think all people should be religious.

20. Was the overseer "poor white trash"? What were some of his rules?

The details of the interview should be reported as accurately as possible in the language of the original statements. An example of material collected through one of the interviews with ex-slaves is attached herewith. Although this material was collected before the standard questionnaire had been prepared, it represents an excellent method of reporting an interview. More information might have been obtained however, if a comprehensive questionnaire had been used.

Sample Interview From Georgia
LULA FLANNIGAN
Ex-slave, 78 years.

"Dey says I wuz jes fo' years ole when de war wuz over, but I sho' does member dat day dem Yankee sojers come down de road. Mary and Willie Durham wuz my mammy and pappy, en dey belong ter Marse Spence Durham at Watkinsville in slav'ry times."

"When word cum dat de Yankee sojers wuz on de way, Marse Spence en his sons wuz 'way at de war. Miss Betsey tole my pappy ter take en hide de hosses down in de swamp. My mammy help Miss Betsey sew up de silver in de cotton bed ticks. Dem Yankee sojers nebber did find our whitefolks' hosses and deir silver."

"Miss Marzee, she wuz Marse Spence en Miss Betsey's daughter. She wuz playin' on de pianny when de Yankee sojers come down de road. Two sojers cum in de house en ax her fer ter play er tune dat dey liked. I fergits de name er dey tune. Miss Marzee gits up fum de pianny en she low dat she ain' gwine play no tune for' no Yankee mens. Den de sojers takes her out en set her up on top er de high gate post in front er de big house, en mek her set dar twel de whole regiment pass by. She set dar en cry, but she sho' ain' nebber played no tune for dem Yankee mens!"

"De Yankee sojers tuk all de blankets offen de beds. Dey stole all de meat dey want fum de smokehouse. Dey bash in de top er de syrup barrels en den turn de barrels upside down."

"Marse Spence gave me ter Miss Marzee fer ter be her own maid, but slav'ry time ended fo' I wuz big 'nough ter be much good ter 'er."

"Us had lots better times dem days dan now. Whatter dese niggers know 'bout corn shuckin's, en log rollin's, en house raisin's? Marse Spence used ter let his niggers have candy pullin's in syrup mekkin' time, en de way us wud dance in de moonlight wuz sompin' dese niggers nowadays doan know nuffin' 'bout."

"All de white folks love ter see plenty er healthy, strong black chillun comin' long, en dey wuz watchful ter see dat 'omans had good keer when dey chilluns vuz bawned. Dey let dese 'omans do easy, light wuk towards de last 'fo' de chilluns is bawned, en den atterwuds dey doan do nuffin much twel dey is well en strong ergin. Folks tell 'bout some plantations whar de 'omans ud run back home fum de fiel' en hev day baby, en den be back in do fiel' swingin' er hoe fo' right dat same day, but dey woan nuffin lak dat 'round Watkinsville."

"When er scritch owl holler et night us put en iron in de fire quick, en den us turn all de shoes up side down on de flo', en turn de pockets wrong side out on call de close, kaze effan we diden' do dem things quick, sompin' moughty bad wuz sho' ter happen. Mos' en lakly, somebuddy gwint'er be daid in dat house fo' long, if us woan quick 'bout fixin'. Whut us do in summer time, 'bout fire at night fer de scritch owl? Us jes' onkivver de coals in de fire place. Us diden' hev no matches en us bank de fire wid ashes evvy night all de year 'roun'. Effen de fire go out, kaze some nigger git keerless 'bout it, den somebuddy gotter go off ter de next plantation sometime ter git live coals. Some er de mens could wuk de flints right good, but dat wuz er hard job. Dey jes rub dem flint rocks tergedder right fas' en let de sparks day makes drap down on er piece er punk wood, en dey gits er fire dat way effen dey is lucky."

"Dem days nobuddy bring er axe in de house on his shoulder. Dat was er sho' sign er bad luck. En nebber lay no broom crost de bed. One time er likely pair er black folks git married, en somebuddy give 'em er new broom. De 'oman she proud uv her nice, spankin' new broom en she lay hit on de bed fer de weddin' crowd ter see it, wid de udder things been give 'em. Fo' thee years go by her man wuz beatin' 'er, en not long atter dat she go plum stark crazy. She oughter ter know better'n ter lay dat broom on her bed. It sho' done brung her bad luck. Dey sent her off ter de crazy folks place, en she died dar."

[File 5]
May 3, 1937

Mr. Edwin Bjorkman, State Director
Federal Writers' Project, WPA
City Hall, Fifth Floor
Asheville, North Carolina

Subj: Ex-slave Narratives

MR. EDWIN BJORKMAN, STATE DIRECTOR

Dear Mr. Bjorkman:

I am quoting a memorandum of Mr. Lomax, folklore editor, regarding the ex-slave stories:

"Of the five States which have already sent in reminiscences of ex-slaves, Tennessee is the only one in which the workers are asking ex-slaves about their belief in signs, cures, hoodoo, etc. Also, the workers are requesting the ex-slaves to tell the stories that were current among the Negroes when they were growing up. Some of the best copy that has come in to the office is found in these stories."

This suggestion, I believe, will add greatly to the value of the collection now being made.

Very   truly   yours,
                    George   Cronyn
Associate Director

CC—Mr. W.T. Couch, Asso. Director Federal Writers'
Project
University Press
Chapel Hill, No. Car.

GWCronyn/a

SENT TO: No. and So. Carolina; Georgia; Alabama; Loui-
siana;
Texas; Arkansas; Kentucky; Missouri; Mississippi;
Oklahoma; Florida

[File 6]
MEMORANDUM
June 9, 1937

TO: STATE DIRECTORS OF THE FEDERAL WRITERS' PROJECT
FROM: Henry G. Alsberg, Director

MEMORANDUM
JUNE 9, 1937

In connection with the stories of ex-slaves, please send in to this office copies of State, county, or city laws affecting the conduct of slaves, free Negroes, overseers, patrollers, or any person or custom affecting the institution of slavery. It will, of course, not be necessary to send more than one copy of the laws that were common throughout the state, although any special law passed by a particular city would constitute worthwhile material.

In addition, we should like to have you collect and send in copies of any laws or accounts of any established customs relating to the admission to your State of bodies of slaves from Africa or other sections, the escape of slaves, etc. Also, we should like to see copies of advertisements of sales of slaves, published offers of rewards for fugitive slaves, copies of transfers of slaves by will or otherwise, records of freeing of slaves, etc. Public records of very particular interest regarding any transaction involving slaves should be photostated and copies furnished to the Washington office.

Furthermore, contemporary accounts of any noteworthy occurrences among the Negroes during slavery days or the Reconstruction period should be copied, if taken from contemporary newspapers. If such records have been published in books, a reference to the source would be sufficient. We have been receiving a large number of extremely interesting stories of ex-slaves. The historic background of the institution of slavery, which should be disclosed with the information we are now requesting, will be very helpful in the execution of the plans we have in mind.

Copies sent to:

Alabama	Georgia	Maryland	North Carolina	Tennessee
Arkansas	Kentucky	Mississippi	Oklahoma	Texas
Florida	Louisiana	Missouri	South Carolina	Virginia
				West Virginia
				Ohio
				Kansas

[File 7]
Notes by an editor on dialect usage in accounts
by interviews with ex-slaves. (To be used in
conjunction with Supplementary Instructions 9E.)

NOTES BY AN EDITOR ON DIALECT USAGE IN ACCOUNTS

Simplicity in recording the dialect is to be desired in order to hold the interest and attention of the readers. It seems to me that readers are repelled by pages sprinkled with misspellings, commas and apostrophes. The value of exact phonetic transcription is, of course, a great one. But few artists attempt this completely. Thomas Nelson Page was meticulous in his dialect; Joel Chandler Harris less meticulous but in my opinion even more accurate. But the values they sought are different from the values that I believe this book of slave narratives should have. Present day readers are less ready for the over-stress of phonetic spelling than in the days of local color. Authors realize this: Julia Peterkin uses a modified Gullah instead of Gonzales' carefully spelled out Gullah. Howard Odum has questioned the use of goin' for going since the g is seldom pronounced even by the educated.

Truth to idiom is more important, I believe, than truth to pronunciation. Erskine Caldwell in his stories of Georgia, Ruth Suckow in stories of Iowa, and Nora Neale Hurston in stories of Florida Negroes get a truth to the manner of speaking without excessive misspellings. In order to make this volume of slave narratives more appealing and less difficult for the average reader, I recommend that truth to idiom be paramount, and exact truth to pronunciation secondary.

I appreciate the fact that many of the writers have recorded sensitively. The writer who wrote "ret" for right is probably as accurate as the one who spelled it "raght." But in a single publication, not devoted to a study of local speech, the reader may conceivably be puzzled by different spellings of the same word. The words "whafolks," "whufolks," "whi'foiks," etc., can all be heard in the South. But "whitefolks" is easier for the reader, and the word itself is suggestive of the setting and the attitude.

Words that definitely have a notably different pronunciation from the usual should be recorded as heard. More important is the recording of words with a different local meaning. Most important, however, are the turns of phrase that have flavor and vividness. Examples occurring in the copy I read are:

durin' of de war
outmen my daddy (good, but unnecessarily put into quotes)
piddled in de fields
skit of woods
kinder chillish

There are, of course, questionable words, for which it may be hard to set up a single standard. Such words are:

paddyrollers, padrollers, pattyrollers for patrollers
missis, mistess for mistress

marsa, massa, maussa, mastuh for master
ter, tuh, teh for to

I believe that there should be, for this book, a uniform word for each of these.

The following list is composed of words which I think should not be used. These are merely samples of certain faults:

1. ah for I
2. bawn for born
3. capper for caper
4. com' for come
5. do for dough
6. ebry, ev'ry for every
7. hawd for hard
8. muh for my
9. nekid for naked
10. ole, ol' for old
11. ret, raght for right
12. sneik for snake
13. sowd for sword
14. sto' for store
15. teh for tell
16. twon't for twan't
17. useter, useta for used to
18. uv for of
19. waggin for wagon
20. whi' for white
21. wuz for was

I should like to recommend that the stories be told in the language of the ex-slave, without excessive editorializing and "artistic" introductions on the part of the interviewer. The contrast between the directness of the ex-slave speech and the roundabout and at times pompous comments of the interviewer is frequently glaring. Care should be taken lest expressions such as the following creep in: "inflicting wounds from which he never fully recovered" (supposed to be spoken by an ex-slave).

Finally, I should like to recommend that the words darky and nigger and such expressions as "a comical little old black woman" be omitted from the editorial writing. Where the ex-slave himself uses these, they should be retained.

This material sent June 20 to states of: Ala., Ark., Fla., Ga.,
Ky., La., Md., Miss., Mo., N.C., Ohio, Okla., Tenn., Texas, Va., and S. Car.

[File 8]
MEMORANDUM
July 30, 1937.

TO: STATE DIRECTORS OF THE FEDERAL WRITERS' PROJECT
FROM: Henry G. Alsberg, Director

MEMORANDUM
JULY 30, 1937.

The following general suggestions are being sent to all the States where there are ex-slaves still living. They will not apply in toto to your State as they represent general conclusions reached after reading the mass of ex-slave material already submitted. However, they will, I hope, prove helpful as an indication, along broad lines, of what we want.

General Suggestions:

1. Instead of attempting to interview a large number of ex-slaves the workers should now concentrate on one or two of the more interesting and intelligent people, revisiting them, establishing friendly relations, and drawing them out over a period of time.

2. The specific questions suggested to be asked of the slaves should be only a basis, a beginning. The talk should run to all subjects, and the interviewer should take care to sieze upon the information already given, and stories already told, and from them derive other questions.

3. The interviewer should take the greatest care not to influence the point of view of the informant, and not to let his own opinion on the subject of slavery become obvious. Should the ex-slave, however, give only one side of the picture, the interviewer should suggest that there were other circumstances, and ask questions about them.

4. We suggest that each state choose one or two of their most successful ex-slave interviewers and have them take down some stories word for word. Some Negro informants are marvellous in their ability to participate in this type of interview. All stories should be as nearly word-for-word as is possible.

5. More emphasis should be laid on questions concerning the lives of the individuals since they were freed.

Suggestions To Interviewers:

The interviewer should attempt to weave the following questions naturally into the conversation, in simple language. Many of the interviews show that the workers have simply sprung routine questions out of context, and received routine answers.

1. What did the ex-slaves expect from freedom? Forty acres and a mule? A distribution of the land of their masters' plantation?

2. What did the slaves get after freedom? Were any of the plantations actually divided up? Did their masters give them any money? Were they under any compulsion after the war to remain as servants?

3. What did the slaves do after the war? What did they receive generally? What do they think about the reconstruction period?

4. Did secret organizations such as the Ku Klux Klan exert or attempt to exert any influence over the lives of ex-slaves?

5. Did the ex-slaves ever vote? If so, under what circumstances? Did any of their friends ever hold political office? What do the ex-slaves think of the present restricted suffrage?

6. What have the ex-slaves been doing in the interim between 1864 and 1937? What jobs have they held (in detail)? How are they supported nowadays?

7. What do the ex-slaves think of the younger generation of Negroes and of present conditions?

8. Were there any instances of slave uprisings?

9. Were any of the ex-slaves in your community living in Virginia at the time of the Nat Turner rebellion? Do they remember anything about it?

10. What songs were there of the period?

The above sent to: Alabama, Arkansas, Florida, Ga., Kentucky, La.,
 Md., Mississippi, Mo., N. Car., Okla., S. Car., Tenn., Texas, Virginia,
 W. Va., Ohio, Kansas, Indiana.

United States. Work Projects Administration

38

[File 9]
MEMORANDUM
September 8, 1937

TO: STATE DIRECTORS OF THE FEDERAL WRITERS' PROJECT
FROM: HENRY G. ALSBERG

MEMORANDUM
SEPTEMBER 8, 1937

It would be a good idea if you would ask such of your field workers as are collecting stories from ex-slaves to try to obtain stories given to the ex-slaves by their parents and grandparents. The workers should try to obtain information about family traditions and legends passed down from generation to generation. There should be a wealth of such material available.

We have found that the most reliable way to obtain information about the age of ex-slaves or the time certain events in their lives took place is to ask them to try to recollect some event of importance of known date and to use that as a point of reference. For instance, Virginia had a very famous snow storm called Cox's Snow Storm which is listed in history books by date and which is well remembered by many ex-slaves. In Georgia and Alabama some ex-slaves remember the falling stars of the year 1883. An ex-slave will often remember his life story in relation to such events. Not only does it help the chronological accuracy of ex-slave stories to ask for dated happenings of this kind, but it often serves to show whether the story being told is real or imagined.

Sent the following states:

Alabama	Maryland	Tennessee
Arkansas	Mississippi	Texas
Florida	Missouri	Virginia
Georgia	N. Carolina	West Virginia
Kentucky	Oklahoma	Ohio
Louisiana	S. Carolina	Kansas
		Indiana

Slave Narratives

www.ingramcontent.com/pod-product-compliance
Lightning Source LLC
Chambersburg PA
CBHW071438040426
42445CB00012BA/1390